# *Storytime*

# *with the Millers*

### by Mildred A. Martin

### Illustrated by Anthony Baker

# *Storytime*

## *with the Millers*

Text and illustrations copyright © 1992, Mildred A. Martin

ISBN 0-9627643-1-0

92-1-92

Green Pastures Press

7102 Lynn Rd.
Minerva, OH 44657

Printed in U.S.A.

# Table of Contents

## The Indians and the Cookies

It was a sunny Sunday afternoon in spring, and the three Miller boys were having a wonderful time playing Indians. Perry, the oldest, was the chief; he had a paper headband adorned with feathers. Joe had Daddy's small hatchet for a tomahawk to cut up wood for the campfire. Mark, with one feather stuck into his blond thatch of hair, was gathering food for the tribe: handfuls of tasty mint leaves from the tea patch, and bark chips for pemmican.

The three boys often played Indians,

but today they had discovered their best campsite yet! Over at the edge of the Miller's yard there was a large bush with a funny name: Bridal Wreath. Under its' leafy branches was the perfect spot for a hideout . . . cool, green, and private. Perry and Joe brought several handfuls of old shingles from the garage, and used them to build a wall up to the bottom branches of the bush.

"Now, nobody can see into our camp, if they go past on the road!" Perry told his brothers happily.

"You know what?" said Joe, crawling from the hide-out again to examine the outside. "This wall of shingles makes our hut look just like a real bark wigwam. An

Iroquois wigwam!"

"Who were the Iroquois?" wondered 5-year-old Mark.

"They were the Indians who lived here in Ohio in the old days. We learned about them in school," Joe replied.

Suddenly the three Indians heard voices. Across the road and up a steep bank of dirt, their eyes followed the sound. There in the neighbor's garden, two teenage boys were hard at work under the hot sun. Pulling weeds and picking up rocks! "Aren't you glad *we* don't believe in working on Sunday?" Perry asked his brothers in a low voice. Giggling, the boys plunged back into the shelter of their wigwam.

But it was too late: the neighbor boys had spotted the Millers, too. "What are you little guys doing?" came a rough shout from the hillside garden. Plop! . . . a large clod of earth hurtled across the road and stuck Perry's shingle wall. Roaring with laughter, the boys tossed another volley of dirt clumps and rocks at the tempting target.

"Hey!" cried Perry, poking his head out of the damaged wigwam. "You stop that, Jason! You almost hit Mark with a rock." But his only answer was a mocking laugh as another dirt clod whistled past, dangerously close to Perry's head.

Hastily grabbing a few possessions, the three Indians scrambled out of their threatened wigwam and sadly retreated to the middle of the yard. Sitting Indian-style on the grass, they held a council. "Those boys are an enemy tribe, and they're shooting missiles at us!" declared Mark.

"Indians don't have missiles, silly," returned Joe.

"We don't want to be *fighting* Indians," Perry said thoughtfully. "How can we make peace with them?" He jumped to his feet. "I know how!" he called, dashing for the house.

"Mom!" Perry exclaimed as he burst into the kitchen. "May I have some cookies to take up to Jason and Matt? Then maybe they will leave us in peace!"

Mother had been observing her sons' problem from the kitchen window. "Why, I think that would be a good idea, Perry!" she answered approvingly. Going to the cupboard she took out some special cookies: big, soft, homemade cookies with gaily colored sprinkles of candy on top. "Be sure you speak politely and nicely," she admonished as she folded the cookies into two white paper napkins.

Joe and Mark watched anxiously as Perry trotted uphill with his offering. "Hey, Jason!" he called in a friendly tone. The big boys looked at him suspiciously, but laid down their hoes and came over. "You boys have been working so hard throwing

dirt at us, I thought you might be hungry! Here are some cookies," Perry said, kindly.

"I bet you've got stones, not cookies," Matt growled.

"No, it's cookies for you!  Here," Perry held out the treat.

"Oh! well, uh, thanks, I guess," stammered the surprised boys.  They returned to their work with their mouths full of cookies, as Perry skipped triumphantly back down the hill.

Soon the Miller tribe of Indians moved into their wigwam once more.  This time they were safe, since they had made enemies into friends . . . and this time they had some cookies to eat, too!

12

*"Children, obey your parents in the Lord, for this is right." Ephesians 6:1.*

## Peter in the Pit

When Peter was three years old, his family moved onto a dairy farm. Peter was excited. There were so many things to see. Best of all was the big barn, with its rows of stalls, interesting tools, and wagons. There were big piles of hay bales and all kinds of big machines.

Peter's dad bought a lot of cows, and some little calves, too. Peter was a bit scared of those big cows! His parents told him he must not get too close to them, because some cows will kick little boys.

13

Peter had four older brothers, and they helped Dad with the chores in the barn. Sometimes Peter helped, too, when they were feeding the calves. At other times Mom wanted him to stay in the house. Then Peter was sad. He wished he would be big enough to milk cows, too.

One afternoon when Peter awoke from his nap he heard the rattle of milk cans and the mooing of cows from the barn. "Mom, may I go to the barn today?" he asked.

"No, Peter," said Mom. "You'd better stay with me. You may go out with me later when I wash the milk buckets."

Peter got out his toy animals and started

14

to make a farm of his own on the floor. He set up four little fences to make a pen for his cows, and pretended to feed them hay. He had a toy horse, too, and made it gallop around the farm.

Soon Peter got tired of playing farm. He wanted to go out to the *real* farm, and see *real* animals.

Mom went upstairs with her arms full of clothes she had washed that day. Peter wandered over to the window and looked out. He could see the barn. He wanted to go out there so much. He got an idea. Surely Mom would not care if he went out and stood in the driveway so he could see the barn better.

Peter looked around. Mom was still upstairs. He put on his boots, then quietly opened the door and went outside. He felt guilty all the time, because he knew he was doing something Mom had said he must not do.

When Peter reached the driveway, he stood there for only a moment. He looked back toward the house. Mom did not call and tell him to come back, so he went on. Soon he had slipped through the door into the milkhouse at the end of the barn.

Peter played in the milkhouse for a minute, then he quietly went on into the main part of the barn. Peter knew he was disobeying, so he did not stop to talk to

Dad and the boys. They did not see that he was in the barn. He stood in the corner and watched as they milked the big cows.

Peter knew where he wanted to go -- to the calf pens. He stood by the pens and watched the little calves for awhile. Then he wanted something else to do.

At the end of the barn was a big manure pit. Peter went there next. He stood on the edge of the pit and wrinkled his nose. "Phew!" he thought. "That manure does not smell good."

Peter found a stick and poked it into the manure. That was fun, so he poked in the manure some more.

Suddenly Peter's foot slipped and he

17

had to take a quick step forward to keep his balance. PLOP! Down went Peter's one foot into the manure. PLOP! Down went the other foot, too.

Peter was so scared he didn't know what to do. The sticky manure was already higher than his knees, and he was sinking deeper all the time. How he wished he had obeyed Mom and stayed in the house. He struggled and tried to walk out of the pit, but that just made him sink deeper.

At last Peter found his voice. "DADDY!" he called. "DAA-DEE! DAAA-DEEEE!"

Peter's big brother, Thomas, was working near the end of the barn. He thought he heard something. Was Peter crying? "No,

it is not Peter," he thought. "Peter is in the house with Mom."

"DAAAA-DEEEE!"

Thomas heard the sound again. He set his bucket down and went in the direction of the sound. When he came to the manure pit, his eyes bulged with shock. There, on top of the manure pit was someone's head. It was his little brother's head. Peter had sunk all the way to his neck, and could no longer scream, but he rolled his frightened eyes at Thomas.

Thomas turned and ran back into the barn. He was crying, too. "Daddy, come quick. Oh, please, come quick!" Then he ran back to the pit.

Dad dropped what he had been doing and came running. He knew something terrible must have happened. When he saw Peter in the pit, he moved even faster. It was not easy to pull him out of the manure, but at last Peter was standing on solid ground again. Oh, how very dirty he was!

Dad and Mom cleaned Peter, then Dad sat with Peter on his lap. He talked to him for a long time. Peter could not understand everything Dad said, but there were two things he understood very well. He had come close to drowning in the manure pit, and it was his disobedience that had caused all the trouble.

Peter would remember that day for the

rest of his life -- the day he learned how serious it can be to disobey.

*"Behold, to obey is better than sacrifice."* I. Samuel
15:22.

## The Best Way to Help

It was Friday afternoon, and six-year-old
Sarah was all excited. They were getting
company for supper! Sarah loved to have
company, especially when there would be
children along. Tonight Preacher Alvins
were coming, and their youngest daughter
was near Sarah's age.

Mom was busy in the kitchen. "What
are you making for supper?" Sarah asked.

"I'm making chicken, with dressing and
potatoes," answered Mom. "And I think I'll
make cupcakes, too."

23

"Cupcakes!" squealed Sarah. She loved cupcakes, and Mom so seldom made them. "I'll peel the potatoes for you," she offered. "Remember, you showed me how last week."

Mom hesitated. "I guess I'll do the potatoes tonight. It will take a lot, and we don't have much time. But you may straighten up the living room. You can put all the toys away, and dust the tops of the furniture."

"Oh, Mom," Sarah grumbled. "I clean up the living room *every* day. I want to help you with supper."

"Sarah, the best way to help me is to do what I tell you," Mom said. "I will let you help me in the kitchen later."

24

Sarah tidied up the living room. She tried to do a good job. She made sure all the toys were picked up, even those in the out-of-the-way places. She straightened the spread on the couch. She dusted the furniture, and set all the old *Family Life*'s straight in the magazine rack. Then she came out into the kitchen.

"What shall I do next?" she asked.

"You may set the table," Mom said. "Set eleven places. Then you may put these cupcake papers into the pans."

Now that was work Sarah enjoyed! That was *really* helping to get ready for company. She set the table neatly. Then she took the package of cupcake papers and put them carefully into the pan, one by one.

Then Baby Daniel let out a cry from the bedroom. He was waking from his nap. Mom brought him downstairs, fed him, and set him on the floor. But he still fussed. He wanted to be held. "Sarah, you will have to take care of him for me now," Mom said. "Please try bringing him a few toys. Play with him, and try hard to keep him happy."

"But Mom," Sarah wailed. "I want to help you!"

Mom laughed. "Sarah, if you take care of Baby Daniel so I can get supper, that *is* helping me. If you don't keep him happy, then I can't work. Remember, the best way to help me is to do what you are told."

Sarah brought a few toys and played with the baby while Mom mixed the cupcake dough. She mixed flour and sugar and other things, and beat it a few minutes. "Now," Mom said. "That's all ready to put into the pans."

Just then Dad came to the door. "I'm sorry, but I need your help for just a few minutes," he said. "I want to move something, and the little boys aren't strong enough to help me."

"All right," Mom said. She hurried out with Dad.

Sarah plopped Daniel on the floor. He began to cry, but she ignored him. This was her chance to really help Mom. She

27

would put the cupcake dough into the pans. "I'll do it quickly, then she will see that I can!" Sarah thought.

Sarah was just barely tall enough to see into the mixing bowl on the counter top. Carefully she took the big spoon and dipped batter into the cupcake pan. She knew enough not to fill it all the way. When she thought she had enough batter in the first one, she went on to the next one. Some of the batter spilled, but she licked it up with her finger. Finally the first pan was filled. Sarah was pleased with herself.

Sarah stood on tiptoes to reach across the filled pan to get the empty one. Then it happened! Her elbow pushed the edge

of the full pan.

KER-PLUNK! The whole pan tipped, spilling all the cupcake batter. Down it went, splashing on the cupboard doors, on the floor, and all over Sarah!

Poor Sarah! She was so sorry. But it was too late. She knew she deserved to be punished. Instead of helping Mom, she had just made another big mess for Mom to clean up. And she had ruined all that precious cupcake batter, too.

Mom's words flashed through Sarah's head. "The best way to help is to do what you are told." How she wished she had obeyed, and not tried to do something Mom had not told her to do.

*"Whatsoever thy hand findeth to do, do it with thy might." Ecclesiastes 9:10.*

## Boys and Toys

"Amos and Joel!" called Mama. "Come here. I have some work for you to do."

Amos and Joel were good workers. They knew that everyone had to do his share of the work. Usually they worked cheerfully and quickly. There were so many things they could do. Amos was five. He could weed in the garden, take care of the baby, and round up the goats when they got loose. He could fold the diapers, and sometimes he even went on carpenter jobs with Daddy.

Joel was three. He could set the table,

run errands, and hand Mama the clothes pins when she hung up the wash. He could water the plants, too.

But there was one job Amos and Joel had to do twice a day, and they did not like to do it. They had to pick up all their toys before lunch and before bedtime. They got so tired of picking up toys. They did not work fast. They poked around. And the longer the job took, the more they hated it.

"Come and pick up your toys now," said Mama. "Then we will walk down to the neighbors and get eggs.

"Oh, goodie, goodie!" the boys cried. They loved to go to the neighbors. They liked to play with the neighbor's children and their toys.

"You will have to hurry," Mama said. "I want to go as soon as I have given baby Micah his bath."

The boys were excited about going to the neighbors'. They picked up toys for a few minutes. But there were so many more toys on the floor, and soon they slowed down. Amos began to tease Joel. Joel grabbed Amos' leg and they started tussling on the floor.

"Boys!" Daddy said. He was working at his desk. "You are not being obedient. Mama told you to pick up your toys."

Amos and Joel got busy. They picked up a few toys, but the job still looked so big. Soon they were playing again. They were playing with the toys instead of picking them up.

Mama called to Daddy. He went into the bedroom to talk to her. "I hate to go without them. They always like to go to the neighbors. But they did not obey," Mama said.

"Go ahead," Daddy said. "I will be here with them. This punishment might help more than a spanking."

Mama dressed the baby to take him outside. She picked up a bag for the eggs. "Good-bye, boys!" she said. "You poked around so long with your work that I have to go without you."

Amos and Joel jumped up and began to cry. They tried to scoop up toys in big handfuls. But they were too late. Soon Mama was walking down the lane.

"I hope you will remember this, so it will not have to happen again," said Daddy. "Do your work right away, then you will be ready to go along next time."

Amos and Joel tried hard to remember. They did not want to be left behind again.

*"A faithful man shall abound with blessings."*
*Proverbs 28:20.*

## Robert Is Responsible

"Dad, may I have a rabbit?" asked Robert. "I want a rabbit of my own, to keep in that old hutch behind our shed."

This was not the first time Robert had asked his parents to let him keep a rabbit. But they always said he was too young.

"A rabbit is a real live animal," Dad said now. "It would need to be fed and cared for every day. If you forgot, your rabbit would suffer."

"Aw, I wouldn't forget to take care of my rabbit," Robert said. "I could give it feed and water every day."

Dad looked across the yard. "Out there is your wagon again," he said sadly. "You forgot to bring it in again, and now it is almost dark. You left some of your toys out in the yard, too."

Robert hung his head. He knew Dad was right. He had a habit of leaving his wagon and other toys wherever he had played with them. Why hadn't he remembered to bring them in before supper? Slowly he went out to get them. "Maybe if I would always put my things away, Dad would let me have a rabbit," he thought.

In the days that followed, Robert often thought of the rabbit he wanted. He tried hard to put his things away without being told.  Soon it was no longer so hard to remember.  Putting things away had become a habit.

Winter came.  Robert played out in the snow a lot.  When it was too cold or too wet to play outside, he played in the house with his little sister Margaret.  He didn't think about asking for a rabbit now.

Spring came.  Robert helped Dad plow the garden.  Then a nice warm day came and Mom wanted to plant the garden.  She was in a hurry.  "I want to plant potatoes, peas, lettuce, and onions before it rains again," she said.  "Robert, you will have to take care of Margaret for me.  You can play with her here in the yard and in the sandbox. But you must watch her all the time, so she doesn't get into trouble. If anything happens, you can call me. But you are responsible for Margaret. It is up to you to see that she does not wander away and get lost."

"Responsible!" Robert thought. "Dad said I have to learn to be responsible before I can have a rabbit. Maybe if I take good care of Margaret, Dad and Mom will say I am old enough to take care of a rabbit."

Margaret was a little more than a year old. She was just starting to walk by herself, and she could say a few words. She really had to be watched every minute, because she could get into all kinds of things.

Mom put Margaret into the sandbox and Robert got in beside her. When Margaret saw Mom hurrying away, she started to cry. "Here, Margaret, you may have this bucket," Robert said kindly. He gave Margaret the nicest bucket and the biggest shovel. He showed her how to scoop up sand. Soon Margaret stopped crying, and was a happy little girl.

When Margaret stepped on Robert's "farm" in the sandbox, Robert remembered not to hit her. When Margaret got tired of the sandbox and crawled out, Robert went along to see where she would go and what she would do. Soon Margaret found a dandelion.  She picked it and wanted to put it into her mouth.

"No, no!" Robert laughed.  "That's not good to eat."

Robert ran to get his wagon, and pulled it back to Margaret.  Margaret stood up, and Robert lifted her into the wagon.  "Ride! Ride!" Margaret said.

Robert pulled the wagon back and forth on the lane for awhile.  Then Margaret was thirsty.  "Dwink!" she begged.  "Dwink!" She pointed to the pump on the porch.

Robert wanted to keep on playing, but he decided he had better give Margaret a drink.  He lifted her from the wagon, and held her hand as they walked to the porch.

Margaret walked *so* slowly, but Robert let her take her time. He pumped water for Margaret and then for himself.

By now Robert was tired of watching Margaret. He wished he could be out working with Dad. He wished Mom would come in from the garden and take Margaret to the house with her. He went over to the swing and sat there, trying to make himself go. Just as the swing had picked up speed, Robert saw Margaret toddling down the hill toward the pasture fence. "I'm responsible for her," Robert remembered. He dragged his feet to stop the swing, and soon he was running after Margaret again.

At last Mom came toward the house.

She looked tired, but when she saw the children, she smiled. "Thank you, Robert, for taking such good care of Margaret!" she said. She took Margaret to the house, changed her diaper, and put her in the highchair with a cracker. Then she quickly fixed dinner, while Robert went out to put his wagon and their other toys away.

After dinner Mom put Margaret to sleep. "I will go out to the garden again," she said. "You may rest here on the couch, and quietly look at these books. When Margaret wakes up, call me quickly."

"Yes, Mom," said Robert. He sat on the couch. He looked at every book in the stack Mom had given him. Then he lay down and fell asleep.

"WAAAH! WAH!" cried Margaret.

Robert sat up and rubbed his eyes. Where was Mom? Then he remembered. He got up from the couch and went to the door. "Mooommm!" he called as loudly as he could. "Margaret's awake."

Mom came hurrying up from the garden. She got Margaret, changed her diaper, and gave her a drink. "I would like to work in the garden for another hour," she said to Robert. "Do you think you can watch Margaret for me again?"

Robert wished he could go along to the garden. That would be so much more fun than taking care of Margaret. But he did not argue. He just said, "I will try."

Once more Mom put Margaret into the sandbox. Margaret was cranky now, and cried for everything Robert had. Finally Robert gave up trying to make a farm, and just played with Margaret. He was pouring sand on Margaret's foot to make her laugh when suddenly he heard a loud noise.

"WOOF! WOOF!"

Robert got up in a hurry and whirled around. There was the neighbor's big, mean dog, coming across the yard, right at them. That dog was not even supposed to be loose!

Robert's heart thumped. He was afraid of that big dog. Once it had jumped up on him and knocked him down. He wanted

to run into the house and shut the door before that big dog got him. But he couldn't! He was responsible for Margaret, and Margaret could not run.

Robert was so scared that his legs shook, but he stood right in front of his little sister. "Go away, you bad dog!" he shouted, waving the sand shovel at him.

The dog stopped, then came closer and barked again. Margaret started to scream. Robert almost jumped up and down in fright. "Go away!" he shouted. This time he threw his shovel at the dog.

Mom heard the noise and came running to see what was wrong. When the dog saw her, he ran away.

48

"Oh, Mom, I don't like that dog!" Robert said. He was crying, too.

"That dog will go home and stay there, I think," Mom said. "I am finished planting now. I will take Margaret into the house with me. You may do whatever you want until suppertime." She smiled at Robert. "Thank you for being such a good helper."

At the supper table that evening, Mom told Dad how Robert had watched Margaret all day, and how he had tried to chase that big dog away.

"Well, well," Dad said, smiling. "I think Robert is growing up."

"Daddy," said Robert, eagerly. "Do you think I am responsible enough to have a rabbit now?"

Dad looked at Mom and Mom looked at Dad. "Maybe you are," Dad said. "We will see."

A few days later Dad went away. When he came back, he had not one, but *two* rabbits for Robert! Robert was very excited. The rabbits were so cute with their soft fur and long, floppy ears. Dad showed him how to feed them and give them clean water. "Remember, they are your rabbits," Dad said. "You are responsible for them."

Robert smiled happily. He was going to try very hard to take care of his rabbits. He knew it should not be hard, now that he had learned to be responsible for other things.

51

*"Bread of deceit is sweet to a man; but afterwards his mouth shall be filled with gravel." Proverbs 20:17.*

## Sammy and the Sugar

Sammy was four, and like all little boys and girls, he liked sweets. He liked ice cream, candy, cookies, and cakes with icing. He wished he could have those things to eat every day. But Sammy's Daddy and Mom were wise. They told him that if he ate too many sweets, he would not be strong and healthy.

Sammy even liked to taste sugar right out of the bag. "Mom, give me some sugar," he would beg when Mom was baking something. Sometimes she let him dip his finger into the sugar bag -- just once.

"Mom, I like sugar so well I could eat a whole bowl full," he said.

"Oh, no," laughed Mom. "If you would try to eat so much sugar, you would not like it any more."

"Oh, yes, I would," Sammy said. He was sure he would always like sugar.

One morning Mom was working in the garden. Sammy helped for a while, but soon he got tired and went to play in the sandbox with his little sister Ruth. Then he felt very hungry.

"Mom, may I have something to eat?" he called.

"Just wait, Sammy," came Mom's voice

from the garden. "It will be time for lunch in half an hour. I want to finish picking these peas.

Sammy knew half an hour was a long time, especially when he was hungry. He played a minute longer, then stood up. He felt *so* hungry. He would go into the house and see if there was anything he could get for himself.

When Sammy entered the kitchen, the first thing he saw was a partly filled bag of sugar on the counter top, where Mom had been using it that morning. Sammy's tummy rumbled with hunger, and a naughty thought popped into his mind. This was his chance! Mom was out in the garden, and he was

going to have as much sugar as he wanted
-- just this once.

Quietly Sammy pushed a chair over to
the cupboard and reached up to get one of
the plastic bowls Mom used to give him
cereal for breakfast. He took a spoon and
placed it in the bowl.

Next he carefully picked up the sugar sack and tipped it over the bowl. The sack was heavy, but Sammy was strong. He let the sugar pour slowly into the bowl until it was nearly full. A pleased smile spread over Sammy's face. All that sugar, and he was going to eat every bite!

Sammy didn't forget to put the chair back at the table where it had been. Then he picked up his bowl of sugar and went quietly out the front door, carrying it in both hands. He went down the porch steps and crawled under the lilac bush. He knew Mom would not be pleased with what he was doing, so he wanted to hide to eat his sugar.

Sammy sat down. He took the bowl on

his lap and ate a big bite of sugar. "Hmmmm," he thought as he crunched the sugar with his teeth and the sweet taste spread through his mouth. Rapidly he gobbled a few more bites, and soon half of the sugar was gone.

Soon it seemed to Sammy the sugar didn't taste as good as it had before. The spoon moved more slowly, and some of his teeth started to hurt. He tried to lick the sugar, rather than chewing it, but it made his mouth feel hot and bitter. Sammy decided he had had enough sugar, but there was still some left in the bowl.

Slowly Sammy ate several more little bites of sugar. Then he heard Mom and Ruth coming in from the garden. Sammy's heart thumped. He took a huge bite of sugar, and nearly choked. He simply had to get rid of the rest of that sugar. He wished he had never taken all that sugar! It was very hard to eat the last bites, but finally he had done it.

Sammy stood up. His tummy hurt. Slowly he walked up the steps and into the house, leaving the bowl and the spoon under the bush. He felt a little dizzy.

"Oh, there you are, Sammy!" Mom said cheerfully. "Come, we are having strawberry shortcake for lunch." She set a bowl of bright red berries at his place, and began sprinkling sugar over them.

Sugar! Sammy's stomach felt as if a

fish were flip-flopping inside it. His face turned pale, "Mom, I - I don't think I want any lunch," he stammered.

"Sammy!" Mom exclaimed. She sounded worried. "Are you sick, or have you done something you shouldn't have?"

Sammy began to cry. Mother was right. He *had* done something he wasn't supposed to, and he *was* sick. That afternoon he felt very sick, so of course he had to tell Mom what he had done.

"I guess I won't need to spank you this time, Sammy," she said. "Being sick is your punishment for eating all that sugar."

Sammy just lay and groaned. His stomach hurt so much. He knew it would be a long time before he would even want to taste sugar again.

*"Let nothing be done through strife or vainglory."*
*Philippians 2:3.*

## Bossy Betty

"Let's play church now!" Betty said to her friends, Susan and Kathy. Susan's and Kathy's families had come to Betty's house for a Sunday evening visit, and the girls were eager to start playing.

"I'd rather play outside," said Susan. "I never tried out your new swing yet."

"Oh, come on, Susan!" Betty insisted. Betty was the oldest child in her family, and she was used to deciding what to play. "I want to play church first. We can swing after supper, before it gets dark." Betty grabbed an armload of hymnbooks from the bookshelf.

"I'm going to bring our baby to hold," Kathy volunteered. "And do you have a purse I can use for a diaper bag?"

The three girls gathered several more of the smaller children, and went out to the front porch, where there was a long, high-backed wooden bench.

"Now, you sit here, Kathy," Betty ordered. "And Jennifer and baby Timmy will be your children."

"I want a baby to hold, too!" begged Susan. "Can I hold Lucy?"

"No! Lucy is *my* little sister!" Betty argued. "But I guess you can have her when

I get up to preach."

"Now, let's start singing," Betty told the children when they were all settled on the bench. "Jesus wants me for a Sunbeam!" she began lustily, and the others joined in.

The children sang "J-O-Y", and "Running Over", and "Jesus Loves Me". Then Kathy's brother Philip heard the singing and came out to the porch. "Can I play, too?" he asked.

"No! We don't want any boys!" Betty said rudely. "This game is only for girls and babies!"

"I could be the preacher," Philip told her. "You need a boy to preach."

"*I'm* going to be the preacher, 'cause I'm

the biggest," said Betty, giving Philip a shove. "You go away."

"But Betty, girls aren't supposed to be preachers," Susan reasoned. "The Bible says so."

"I don't care!" cried Betty. "This is my game, and I don't want him in it! Sit still, Lucy," she added, squeezing her little sister tighter as she tried to climb down from Betty's lap.

But the other girls had had enough. "You're just too bossy, Betty," Susan declared.

"Bossy Betty!" Kathy giggled. "That sounds right."

"Bossy Betty!" "Bossy Betty!" Philip and Jennifer chimed in.

Betty's face burned, and tears came to her eyes. Choking back sobs, she turned and ran. Where could she hide? There! Nobody was in her bedroom. Betty slammed the door shut and flopped down on her bed, crying hot tears of anger and shame.

Suddenly Mother was sitting on the bed beside her. "Betty, what is wrong?" she asked quietly.

"They - they called me 'Bossy Betty'!" the little girl wept. "They don't want to play like I say!"

"Betty, sit up," her mother said firmly. "I know it makes you feel upset if the other children call you names. But it sounds like you *were* being bossy. When you have guests, you must play what they want to play. And you should have let Philip be the preacher. Now blow your nose, and come into the kitchen."

Mother stood up and looked out the window. "The other girls are playing happily on the swing now," she told Betty. Come and help me put the food on the table, and after supper you can try again to play nicely with your friends."

Meekly, Betty followed her mother to the kitchen. "After supper I will let the other girls choose what to play," she decided to herself. "I don't want to be 'Bossy Betty' anymore!"

69

*"Thou shalt honor the face of the old . . ."*
*Leviticus 19:32.*

## Going to Grandma's

We are going to visit Grandmother Miller this afternoon," Dad said one Sunday. Then he added, "Old people sometimes don't like noise, so I want you children to be quiet and respectful."

"What is respectful?" asked four-year-old David.

"When you are quiet and polite, that is being respectful," Dad explained.

"Will Grandma have toys for us to play with?" asked Susan, who was three.

"She may not have many," Mother said.

70

"She lives in a little house, and no children live with her. We will take one doll along for Susan, and a toy car for David. Then we want you to sit quietly and play with them."

Soon the family was on the way. "Grandma Miller is really my grandmother," Dad told David and Susan. "She is your great-grandmother."

"Is she very old?" asked Susan.

"Yes," replied Dad. "She is probably the oldest person you have ever seen. When people get very old, sometimes their bodies don't work well anymore. That is why Grandma Miller is in a wheelchair. Her legs are not strong enough for her to walk anymore."

Susan thought about how easy it was for her to walk. What if her legs would be too old and weak to walk?

"Old people have lived a long time, and learned a lot," Dad went on. "That is why we must be respectful to them and listen to what they have to say."

Soon they were at Grandma's house. Dad knocked on the door.

"Come in!" Grandma Miller called cheerfully.

David and Susan stepped quietly into the room and stared at Grandma, sitting there in her wheelchair. They shook hands politely, then sat down to listen to the

grownups' talk.

Susan rocked her doll for a while, then carried her quietly around the room to show her the flowers. Suddenly she saw a very big and pretty flower. "Mom! What kind of flower is this?" she asked. "It has three big, bright flowers."

Mother did not answer right away. She put her hand on Susan's arm and went right on talking to Grandma.

Susan hung her head, feeling ashamed. She had been so excited, she had not noticed that Mom was talking.

At last Mom turned to her and said, "What did you want, Susan?"

"What kind of flower is that?" she asked,

pointing. "It is very pretty."

"That is a gloxinia," Grandma answered with a smile. "I am glad you like it."

Just then David's toy car went Zoom! Zoom! Zoom! across the floor. He forgot about being quiet and respectful.

"Shhh! David, not so loud," Dad said.

David made his car go more quietly. It was more fun to zoom loudly, but he wanted to be respectful.

After what seemed like a long time to Susan and David, Dad said it was time to go home.

"Wait a minute," said Grandma. "These children were so nice and quiet, I want to give them something." She wheeled her chair out to the kitchen, and was soon back with a little bag. She gave it to Susan.

"Thank you!" Susan said. She peeped into the bag, and let David look, too. "Four big cookies!" she said out loud. "We can each have one for supper, and Mom and Dad, too."

Grandma smiled. "Yes, that is what they are for," she said.

When they were all in the car and on the way home, Dad said, "Thank you, children, for being so nice and quiet. Grandma appreciated it, and we did, too."

"I forgot once and interrupted Mom when she was talking," Susan said, hanging her head. "I am sorry."

"I forgot, too, and made my car go loudly," David said. "I'm sorry."

"You tried hard, didn't you?" Mom said. "We are glad you are learning to be respectful."

Susan felt good inside. Being respectful made her happy.

*"A righteous man regardeth the life of his beast, but the . . . wicked are cruel." Proverbs 12:10.*

# Timmy's Goat

Toot, toot! Sounded the horn as the Miller's black station wagon pulled into the lane.

"Daddy's home!" Timmy shouted, running across the yard. "But, oh!" his eyes grew round with surprise. "*What* is that in the back of the car?"

A funny little face was peering out the window. Long floppy ears, bright yellow-brown eyes, tiny stubs of horns on top -- and then a second little face popped up beside the first! "Goats! Two baby goats in the car?"

Timmy gasped, hardly able to believe his eyes.

Daddy Miller opened his car door and stepped out. "Surprise!" he told Timmy with a big grin. "Uncle Leonard gave us these two kids, since I have been doing his chores for him while his broken leg heals. We put them into feed sacks for the trip home." He opened the rear door of the station wagon as he spoke. Each little goat was in a feed sack, with the draw-string tied around his neck! They looked so funny.

"Ba-a-ah!" they cried as Daddy lifted them out one by one. Gently he took off the feed sacks and set them free on the grass.

Timmy's big brother Peter heard the noise, and came out of the house. "Kids!" he cried excitedly. "Are they for us?"

"Yes, boys. These kids will be yours, if you take good care of them," Daddy said. "There is one for each of you."

"I want this one!" Timmy declared. "With the brown spots. I will call him Buster."

"You boys will need to give your goats a

bottle of milk every morning and evening, because they are still very young," Daddy told them. He took two black rubber objects from his pocket. "Here are some special nipples that are just the right size for kids; we will put them onto pop bottles, and that's what you can use to feed milk to your pets."

Peter and Timmy took good care of their little goats. They fed them lots of milk, hay, and grain-pellets. Soon Buster and Blackie, Peter's goat, grew big and strong. The boys had a lot of fun playing with their pet goats!

One day Timmy had an idea. "I wonder if I could ride on my goat's back?" he said to Peter. "Buster is so big now, I'm sure he could carry me!"

"You'd better ask Daddy first," Peter told him.

"Yes, I believe you could ride on your goat, if he will let you," Daddy said, looking at the slender six-year-old. "Peter mustn't try it, though. He would be too heavy."

"Yay!" Timmy cheered happily. Quick as a flash, he was back outdoors and running to the pasture where the goats were grazing.

"Buster! Buster! Ba-a-ah!" called Timmy, and there was an answering "Ba-a-ah!" as the goat trotted to meet him. Buster looked eagerly at his young master as if to say, "What did you bring for me to eat?"

"It's not feeding time yet, Buster," said Timmy, stroking his pet's neck. "I'm going to teach you a new trick, instead." Carefully he took hold of the goat's horns, and climbed onto his back. "Now, Buster, Giddyap!" he ordered.

Buster turned his head to stare in surprise at Timmy. "Ba-a-ah!" he grunted, and tried to shake off the strange weight on his back. "No, Buster!" cried Timmy. "Giddyap and go!" But Buster would not go forward.

Timmy tried again and again, but his goat would not do what he wanted. Buster kept trying to shake him off. He dug his hooves stubbornly into the ground and refused to move. Sometimes he would take a few steps backward, but he never moved in the right direction!

Timmy was getting hot and frustrated. "I know what I need," he decided at last. "I need a *whip* to make this goat go!" He ran over to the fence row and chose a tall, tough-looking weed. "This will teach Buster to go," Timmy muttered as he began to pull. But the big weed was as stubborn as the goat! Timmy set his feet wide apart and pulled with all his might. Suddenly the big weed came bursting up out of the ground, and Timmy sat down with a hard thump. "Owww!" he cried as he stood up, rubbing his sore bottom.

"*Now* that goat had better go," Timmy growled as he stalked across the field, stripping the leaves from his switch.

"Giddyap, Buster!" he commanded sternly as soon as he was seated on the goat's back once more. But again the bewildered Buster would not move forward, so Timmy raised his switch and brought it down smartly across the goat's rump. "Ba-a-ah!" cried Buster. Down went his head, up came his back. Before Timmy knew what was happening, he had hit the ground again -- landing on his head this time!

"You mean goat!" Timmy cried as he got to his feet. "I'll teach you not to buck me off!" Gripping the switch, he started after Buster, who was dancing around nervously just out of reach.

"Wait, Timmy!" Daddy's deep voice

stopped him. "What is going on?" Timmy turned to see his father standing at the fence.

"Oh, Daddy!" wailed Timmy. "Buster just won't *go* when I sit on his back! And when I whipped him, he bucked me off!"

"Whipping your goat won't work, I'm afraid," Daddy told Timmy. "Buster will just get scared of you if you treat him like that. He will soon learn to think, 'Here comes the boy that hurts me,' and will run away when he sees you."

"How can I train him, then?" Timmy asked, sadly.

"Well," his father encouraged, "I'm sure you can figure out something. You will need to think of a way to make Buster *want* to go forward. How about using something he likes to eat?"

Timmy sat down in the warm, sunny pasture to think. Suddenly his eyes brightened. Jumping up, he ran to the big old maple tree that stood beside the pasture fence. Several branches hung low enough to reach, and sometimes Daddy would break off a small bunch of leaves as a treat for the goats. Now Timmy picked a leafy branch about 3 feet long, and went to look for Buster once more.

"Ba-a-ah! Come, Buster!" he called. This time the goat came more cautiously. But when he saw what Timmy had, he

88

trotted faster!  Timmy let Buster nibble a few of the leaves, while he climbed onto the goat's back.  Then he held the branch just out of reach in front of Buster's face. "Giddyap, Buster!" he ordered excitedly. And now, eager for more of the delicious maple leaves, Buster moved forward at last!

"So, I finally got a good ride," Timmy reported to the rest of the Millers at supper, "by using kindness instead of a whip!  Now Buster and I can have even more fun together."

*"In like manner also, that women adorn themselves in modest apparel." I. Timothy 2:9.*

## It's Safer To Be Plain

Slowly the screen door swung shut behind Laura, and slowly she made her way into the warm kitchen. Mama was just taking a panful of hot golden-brown cookies from the oven, but today Laura hardly noticed the delicious smell.

"Hello, Laura!" her mother cheerfully greeted the first grader as she dropped her new lunch box on the counter. "What's wrong with my sunshiny girl today? Are you tired of school, after only 3 days?"

"No," the six-year-old replied unhappily.

"I like the teacher, and I like Math and learning to read. But . . . " her voice trailed off.

"But what, Laura?" Mama encouraged her.

"Well, the other girls said my dress isn't pretty," Laura grumbled. "It's too plain!" She looked down at the new blue school

dress which had made her so happy when Mama first finished it.

"I said, 'My dress is, too, pretty!' But Becky and Sarah laughed and said it was just an Amish dress. Sarah said, 'Look, I have ruffles on my skirt and a bow on top. Your dress doesn't have anything!' And Jennifer's dress had pretty little dots all through the cloth; and Becky's Mom makes fancy stitches all around her neck and sleeves . . . she said it was called 'a-broidery'."

Laura looked sadly at her mother. "Why do we have to wear clothes that are plain?" she asked.

Mama sat down and lifted her daughter onto her lap. Smiling down into the troubled little face, she said softly, "Laura, sometimes it *is* hard to be different. But that's the way life is: we need to do what we believe is right, even though others don't. Wearing plain, simple clothing makes it easier for us to serve the Lord, because we don't need to waste a lot of time and money on fancy things. And anyway, it's safer to be plain."

"What do you mean, Mama?" Laura asked, snuggling closer to her mother.

"Well, that reminds me of a story that was written by a wise man named Aesop, many hundreds of years ago."

"Tell it!" begged Laura.

"Well," Mama began, "Once a large, orange and black butterfly came to rest on the branch of a tree. As it sat lazily fanning those bright wings in the sunshine, suddenly it noticed a moth already on the branch! The gray moth clung to the branch with wings folded down, looking just like the bark on the tree.

"How plain you are," the butterfly said mockingly, fluttering her own golden wings. "You have no color at all! I almost didn't see you were here. Don't you wish you were beautiful, like me?" But just as she spoke, a small hawk spied the bright wings. Swooping down from the sky, he seized her in his sharp talons . . . . and that was the end of the beautiful, boastful butterfly.

"But the plain, gray little moth sat safely

on her branch.  The hawk hadn't noticed her."

Laura giggled.  "I guess it really is safer to be plain," she admitted, sliding down from her mother's lap.  "I'll go change out of my new dress now, so I won't get it dirty . . . and then may I have some cookies, Mama?"

*Also by Mildred A. Martin:*

## Wisdom and the Millers
*(Proverbs for Children)*
*25 chapters illustrating great truths*
*of life in story form. Ages 6-13.*

*Inquire at your favorite book dealer or write to:*

**Green Pastures Press**
*7102 Lynn Rd. N.E.*
*Minerva, OH 44657*